MW00366759

PRAISE FOR THE NETWORKING BOOK

It is with great honor that I write these words. My dear friend Simone was one of the pioneers in the scientific approach to the now extremely popular discipline of networking, and she was trailblazing techniques for practical applications of networking before almost anyone else. With this book (her fourth, the first three being bestsellers) she takes your networking skills one big step further. Welcome to Networking 2.0!

Mogens Nørgaard, serial IT entrepreneur/CEO, International lecturer

"Simone's great passion is networking. She is constantly on the lookout for new trends that can be utilised in her own work and shared with her network. Everyone has a network but few people bring it into play like Simone. Her thoughts and tips about networking have developed and benefited our business."

Michael Krogh, CEO KplusK

"As a speaker Simone is a fantastic communicator. Through her keenness and analytical talent, she quickly establishes customer needs and transforms them into concrete knowledge that is brilliantly communicated to her audience. Her passion for networking is obvious and leaves her audience in a state of euphoria."

Ernst A. Jønsson, IOOF - The Independent Order of Odd Fellows

"If you want a company that is on the move and striving to be successful, the board of directors and the CEO should give greater priority to networking in their business strategy. It is going to be an even more decisive factor during the next few years. Simone has the competence and the tools to help your business implement networking."

Svend Randers, CEO, AL Finans

"I can warmly recommend this compact and intensive introduction to the discipline of networking... If you have been hesitating to take the plunge into the networking scene, Simone's book is designed to help you. This is a pleasurable self-help book that is definitely one to consider if you are looking for some advice on how to develop your skills as a professional networker"

Jeanette Mørk, Marketing Manager, Lawfirm HjulmandKaptain

TO MY AMAZING
DAUGHTER ANDREA

THE
NETWORKING
BOOK

50 WAYS TO DEVELOP STRATEGIC RELATIONSHIPS

SIMONE ANDERSEN

LONDON   NEW YORK   SHANGHAI
MADRID   BARCELONA   BOGOTA
MEXICO CITY   MONTERREY   BUENOS AIRES

Published by
LID Publishing Ltd
One Adam Street
London
WC2N 6LE
United Kingdom

31 West 34th Street, Suite 8004,
New York, NY 10001, US

info@lidpublishing.com
www.lidpublishing.com

A member of:

www.businesspublishersroundtable.com

All rights reserved. Without limiting the rights under copyright reserved, no part
of this publication may be reproduced, stored or introduced into a retrieval
system, or transmitted, in any form or by any means (electronic, mechanical,
photocopying, recording or otherwise) without the prior written permission of
both the copyright owners and the publisher of this book.

© Simone Andersen, 2015
© LID Publishing Ltd, 2015
Reprinted 2015, 2017

Printed in the Czech Republic by Finidr

ISBN: 978-1-910649-00-8

Cover and page design: Laura Hawkins
English Language Supervisor: Erik Knudsen

FOR OTHER TITLES IN THE SERIES...

CONCISE ADVICE LAB

SMALL BOOKS: BIG IDEAS

CLEVER CONTENT, DYNAMIC IDEAS, PRACTICAL
SOLUTIONS AND ENGAGING VISUALS –
A CATALYST TO INSPIRE NEW WAYS OF THINKING
AND PROBLEM-SOLVING IN A COMPLEX WORLD

conciseadvicelab.com

CONTENTS

INTRODUCTION

If you want to give your working life or your personal life a boost; if you want things to happen, your dreams to come true or your ambitions to be achieved – the only way to accomplish this is to have a good network of contacts.

You may already have an active network, but need to revitalize it with new contacts and opportunities. You may have a network that has grown so complex and chaotic that it has become inefficient. Or maybe you have a network that is too small because the process of building one and becoming a good networker seems difficult and out of your comfort zone.

Unfortunately, some people consider networks and networking pure exploitation and nepotism. But when you begin to realize how networking can be the key to releasing your own and other people's potential and that it is more a matter of knowledge sharing and establishing relations, most people want to have a share in the knowledge, the benefits and, not least, the human enrichment that is a part of networking.

A SUPER NETWORKER ONCE CAME UP WITH THE FOLLOWING ASSERTION: "HAVING A GOOD NETWORK IS LIKE BEING GENUINELY PRESENT IN YOUR LIFE."

It is well-documented that what we want and desire comes more easily when we know how to establish good relationships with the people around us. However, many people find it hard to establish a good network and to have to take on other people in networking.

It is estimated that up to 90% of people find it awkward and hugely challenging to contact people they do not know. So you are absolutely not alone in finding this daunting – most people you come across feel exactly the same way.

However, it is a fact that networks and networking make life easier, and it is not until you have established a good team of people around you that you can feel competent and qualified.

This book is designed to help you create that kind of life. It is going to offer guidance and direction on how to establish a network and how to become a skilled and well-liked networker.

This book also shows you how to save time and reach your goals efficiently by implementing the new networking strategy: Networking Version 2.0.

Much of the advice is based on visual expression – a fast and efficient way to understand and skillfully integrate networking into your world. Each idea is shown on one spread, explained in a simple manner and accompanied by a short exercise to help you apply it to your situation.

BASICALLY, NETWORKING IS A GREAT NUMBER OF EXCHANGES OF SERVICES AND THE MOST PRECIOUS INSURANCE IN YOUR PRIVATE LIFE AND YOUR BUSINESS LIFE.

For consideration: it is your ability to establish relationships and networks that gives you influence and power.

Good luck with all the new opportunities that will open up to you and in your career!

PART ONE

PREPARING TO NETWORK

A WORD
ON PREPARING TO NETWORK

For many people, networking – and especially face-to-face networking - is a majorly challenging task.

It is seen as extremely unpleasant to be forced out of your comfort zone and to have to approach people you do not know.

On the other hand, most people know instinctively that exciting opportunities might open up to them if they had the courage to go for it. They could be talking openly about their hopes and visions, experiencing the benefits of knowledge sharing and feeling the joy of helping other people progress in their lives and careers.

We all love to be successful and networking offers a host of genuine opportunities.

It is all about:
- Opening your eyes to the benefits that are inherent in a good and relevant network
- Acquiring practical skills like managing your body language, being a good communicator and spelling out wishes and opinions
- Making networking a natural part of your everyday life

NETWORKING IS NOT ABOUT DEVELOPING AS MANY RELATIONSHIPS AS POSSIBLE OR HANDING OUT LARGE QUANTITIES OF BUSINESS CARDS. NETWORKING IS ABOUT ADDING QUALITY TO THE RELATIONSHIPS YOU CHOOSE TO ENTER.

This book addresses both beginners and skilled networkers, and the tools can be used in private, as well as business, contexts.

Would you like to open up to opportunities in your life?
OK, keep reading!

1: A KICK IN THE RIGHT DIRECTION

Many people who plan to build a network of contacts hesitate and think: I would like to get started, but I need to read a few books on networking, to have more time available and to lose a few kilos – then I will be ready.

Or they play it safe by referring to a very common, but widespread, misunderstanding; that introverted people cannot possibly be good networkers. They can – and they can even become some of the world's best. Several of the world's largest and most successful companies have introverted CEOs.

- There are too many poor excuses because most people know that they can expect to face numerous challenges. Many fear they are going to suffer yet another failure.

- Fear is located in the primitive part of the brain, and it reacts by rejecting new ideas. That is why we have to force ourselves to seek a different part of the brain with access to joy and energy. Through the knowledge and the exercises brought up in this book, you will be able to do just that.

- Networking has to be tried out, reflected upon, tried out again and reconsidered, and along the road, you will learn what works especially well for you. Your code to becoming a good networker has to be cracked, and basically, it is all about boosting the skills and qualities you already possess and learning a few simple techniques to make these resources efficient.

- Excuses are often queuing up, but the truth is that the perfect time and ideal circumstances will never appear at the same time.

**"YOUR MIND IS LIKE A PARACHUTE.
IT ONLY WORKS WHEN IT IS OPEN." UNKNOWN**

EXERCISE: Get Down To It!

1. *Decide to make networking a part of your everyday life*

2. *Drop the negative views you have of networking*

3. *Visualize the benefits networking can bring you*

Use this book chronologically: one tip a day, and you are on the right path to success. Or use it as a reference when you face a challenge.

2: WHY NETWORKS AND NETWORKING?

- Sometimes it is easier to identify the advantages of networking by focusing on what you lose by **not** having an active network.

- In a worst-case scenario you will see others grab the best jobs, win promotions, attract exciting new customers and become successful.

- In an effective network, your contacts will be loyal to you, recommend you for jobs and to customers and friends, and share knowledge with you. They will offer you influence and opportunities.

- An ideal network is a place in which you can be yourself and be respected for your attitude and behaviour. It is a place in which, through words, behaviour and attitude, you are able to cultivate your untapped potential and experience the joy of enriching others' lives and helping them exploit their own potential.

- In short, you have to get going – whether you start from scratch or do some serious work on your current network.

NETWORK VERSUS NETWORKING
- **A NETWORK** IS SOMETHING YOU ESTABLISH
- **NETWORKING** IS WHEN YOU DEVELOP AND MAKE USE OF YOUR NETWORK

EXERCISE:

1. *If you have never before worked on the task of building relationships, describe in three bullet points, what you would like to achieve through networking.*

2. *If you are already a networker, describe in three bullet points what you would like to achieve through a more goal-orientated approach to networking.*

3: NETWORKING - IN YOUR PERSONAL LIFE

- People who are successful are often regarded as "lucky".

- Richard Wiseman[1] has written the book *The Luck Factor*, and a recurring conclusion in his research is that people with relevant networks feel lucky to a much greater extent than people with limited networks or no networks at all.

- Lucky people seem to get attractive jobs, have longer partnerships and lead satisfying lives. People with limited networks find life more difficult, and generally, there are no easy solutions offered to them.

- Wiseman's research shows that 50% of people feel both lucky and unlucky in their daily lives; 25% feel distinctly unlucky and never fortunate, while the remaining 25% feel fortunate and satisfied.

- A related question Wiseman addresses is whether we are born lucky or unlucky. His conclusion is that luck is a state of mind. People who said they felt lucky were often exposed to incidents that were a lot worse than those experienced by people who felt unlucky.

- People who feel lucky and successful seem to share a common characteristic: they have extensive, efficient networks. Despite facing serious difficulties they have turned their challenges into something positive.

EXERCISE:

1. *Analyze yourself: are you occasionally lucky or unlucky, or are you generally lucky or unlucky?*

2. *Ask the people around you how they see you.*

3. *Consider how you tackle adversity. Do you belong to the "I am never successful" category?*

4. *Is it about time you reassessed your mindset?*

[1]Richard Wiseman: The Luck Factor - The Scientific Study of the Lucky Mind, Cornerstone 2004.

4. NETWORKING - AS AN EMPLOYEE

- It is estimated that 70-80% of all job vacancies are filled through networking.

- Networking and establishing relationships are expected to be among the most important growth areas over the next few years.

- Lynda Gratton[2], Professor at London Business School, has researched the workplace of the future, and she believes technology will force us to specialize further. The ongoing development of technology calls for employees to share their competences further. In the future, we should be able to share knowledge and networks with other specialists. In other words, there will be an emphasis on our ability to combine networks and know-how.

- If you are looking for a job, or would like to change jobs, you should be aware that networking is top of the agenda with many employers. Many companies are conscious that professional skills can be acquired relatively fast, whereas professional networking competences may take some time. So if you can boast a relevant network in your CV, you may end high up on the list of attractive applicants.

- If you remember to use your network in your daily routines, for example, by recommending candidates for jobs in your company, new business partners, customers or access to productive know-how, you will probably not be the first employee to be let go if your company decides to downsize or 'trim the fat'.

EXERCISE:

1. *If you are in employment: how could you, through your network, provide new competences and opportunities to your workplace?*

2. *If you are job-seeking: study the map of your network (See tip 7). Identify contacts who could be worthwhile references in a job application or during an interview.*

[2] Lynda Gratton, included by The Times in the TOP 20 greatest contemporary business strategists. Lynda Gratton investigates: The Future of Work: http://www.lyndagratton.com/uploads/BSR%20-%20LG%20investigates%20the%20FOW.pdf

5. NETWORKING – IN THE COMPANY SETTING

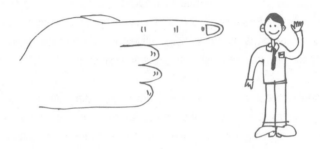

APPOINT CORPORATE AMBASSADORS
- In most companies, it is the head of the organization who does the hard outward-orientated work in terms of building relationships, alliances and knowledge sharing. However, managing directors rarely see themselves as skillful networkers, and that is why they seldom consider passing on this competence to other members of staff.

- External networking: consider the potential growth and development opportunities that could come from making staff external network ambassadors.

- Internal networking: knowledge sharing and establishing internal relationships will be crucial to the workplace of the future. So it is essential to create an attractive setting that makes it easy for employees to build relationships and share knowledge.

- It is the company's duty to make employees aware of the positive outcomes they could achieve through knowledge sharing and building relationships.

- If employees recognize the importance of activating the ambassador concept, the growth potential for the organization, and themselves, will be enormous.

EXERCISE:

If you want to make employees efficient ambassadors it is often necessary to change their mindset and offer introductions to the principles of knowledge sharing and relationship building. It is all about:

1. *Mapping the individual worker's network and its potential*

2. *Drawing employees' attention to the advantages of the new mindset*

3. *Offering employees the tools for knowledge sharing and establishing relationships*

6. TYPES OF NETWORK

It is important to identify the resources to which you have access and where you can find them. Generally, you can work with three different types of network:

YOUR PROFESSIONAL NETWORK
- Here, you find people with whom you share professional interests. These are often like-minded people with similar educations, job functions and workplaces.
- It is an important network because it offers you feedback and the security you need to feel at ease at work and in your personal life.

YOUR BUSINESS NETWORK
- This network includes relationships outside of your professional network. These contacts are relevant people too, but may have different approaches to business matters than those in your professional network. They represent multiple competences and resources.
- The contacts in your business network are important in your personal life, your career and your company, partly because

these relationships tend to be the ones that direct you towards your goals, and partly because development and progress are often generated through co-operation with people who possess different competences and perspectives to you.

YOUR PERSONAL NETWORK

- Here, you find your family and friends – people who are close to you.
- If you only want to use your network for personal development, this network should be your priority.
- If you are focusing on your professional development, you should not spend too much energy on this network as, in my experience, efficient professional help is seldom found in a personal network.

IT IS NATURAL TO SPEND TIME WITH LIKE-MINDED PEOPLE, BUT DEVELOPMENT AND RESULTS ARE OFTEN ACHIEVED BY CO-OPERATING WITH DIFFERENT TYPES OF PEOPLE, WITH DIFFERENT SKILLS AND QUALITIES.

EXERCISE:

1. *In which types of network do you have active contacts? Name the last two contacts who helped you on the way towards your goals.*

2. *In which of the three types of network were these relationships established? Are they good enough for you and your ambitions?*

7. MAP AND VISUALIZE YOUR NETWORK

In order to find useful people and become aware of the strengths and shortcomings of your present network you should map it like this:

- **In the inner circle** you write the names of the most important and most active people in your business or private life. They could be mentors, people who back you up and support you. And don't forget people with whom you disagree. They are often a helpful alternative to the 'yes-people', who never challenge you. Your inner circle will typically comprise two-to-six people.

- **In the middle circle** you find contacts who are professionally relevant to you, although they are not in your confidence to the same degree as those in the inner circle. These could be people you have met at conferences, in networking environments or present or former colleagues and friends from university. In other words, people you have met and who are still relevant to you. Your middle circle will typically hold 10-30 people who you know quite well. You can contact them, and they will know who you are.

- **In the outer circle** you place potential sources of inspiration: people you know of, may have run into and who you would like to get to know better. You can easily have 50-plus contacts in this circle, but too many will make things chaotic. So clearing up this circle on a regular basis is critical.

- Review your network at least once a year.

EXERCISE:

Spend a few hours on this task.

1. *Draw the three circles on a large piece of paper. Start from the centre writing the names of the contacts with whom you have the closest personal or private relationship.*

2. *Work your way chronologically through your school days, your time of study and your business career.*

3. *When your network is fully mapped, you will have a working tool available for your future journey.*

4. *Consider: do I have a network of contacts who are compatible with my ambitions?*

8. ONLINE NETWORKING

- In addition to physical networks, where we meet face-to-face, there are plenty of opportunities for online networks via social media platforms such as Facebook, LinkedIn, Twitter, YouTube, Instagram and blogs.

- Social networks have their specific strengths when it comes to researching contacts and seeing the big picture. Likewise, they are good for making initial contact with people and for maintaining relationships.

- Social media is an efficient shop window, providing visibility. Here we can exhibit ourselves and our brand and reveal the person or the company we would like to be in the eyes of the public.

- Social media is a tool enabling visibility and can open a window to the world for you. However, you should be careful not to be too obtrusive and aggressive here as many people consider it bad networking form.

- Provide your social media contacts with good value, offer them guidance and direction. This is how the media works, but it is also the best way to sell yourself and your company. When you offer value, you are much more likely to gain something valuable in return.

EXERCISE:

Sometimes we spend too much time on social media.

Go through your contacts and consider deleting some from your network if you spend too much time reading irrelevant material.

9. ESTABLISH VISIBILITY ON SOCIAL MEDIA

Improve your profiles. Be sure they are attractive and complete. Think about your keywords. What do users have to type into search engines to find people like you? Include the relevant keywords in your profiles.

VISIBILITY ON SELECTED SOCIAL MEDIA

LinkedIn:
- Your professional identity is especially important here.
- You can upload your CV, describe your achievements and release details of meetings and events.
- Join groups so that you indicate what your expertise and interests are all about.
- LinkedIn is a good platform to keep updated if you are looking for a job or want to change jobs.

Facebook:
- Here you can post personal status updates and comment on your friends' contributions.

- If you have a company Facebook account, you can boost your adverts, events and highlight your achievements by paying to be promoted to a defined target audience. This ensures greater visibility and spreads your messages further.

YouTube:
- Use videos to introduce yourself, your company and your products. Skip traditional advertising and go into storytelling so that it does not look like direct selling. Use Facebook, Twitter and LinkedIn to signpost people to your YouTube channel.
- An efficient way to boost your visibility on social media is to share your knowledge generously and comment frequently on network activities. This is proof that you respect your fellow networkers and their competences.

EXERCISE:

1. *Do you have up-to-date profiles on social media? Does your personal or company profile provide an accurate picture of you and your business?*

2. *Focus on your keywords – the search words Google and other search engines use to identify you.*

3. *Opt for simplicity when developing your brand. Give priority to a few essential characteristics. Most people get confused and exasperated when they are presented with too much information.*

4. *Pictures have a wide and instant appeal and will tell a story about you.*

10. FACE-TO-FACE NETWORKING OFFLINE

- Online social networks have their strengths when it comes to researching new contacts, providing an overview of you or your company and maintaining contacts.

- However, face-to-face meetings are still very important, as digital media cannot convey good eye contact, a warm handshake or an accommodating attitude.

- Face-to-face interaction helps build stronger, more productive and more mutually beneficial relationships.

- We are social beings who gather information through our senses. So we need to analyze our surroundings before we allow strangers to interact in our world.

- A new contact's character has to be decoded: who are you, what signals do you send, would I like to invest in this relationship at all?

- In brief, we have to accept one another on several levels because this acceptance is critical for establishing relationships.

- Meeting someone in person makes it easier to remember them than if we interact with them remotely.

- This book primarily focuses on developing face-to-face relationships as this form of contact is critical for networking, and because face-to-face interaction is an enormous challenge for many people.

EXERCISE:

1. *Register your reactions next time you enter a room full of strangers: do you feel uncomfortable? Do you feel flushed, is your heart beating fast? Or do you feel on top of the world, full of energy and "get up and go"? Your honest reaction is very important when you read the rest of this book.*

11. HOW MANY CONTACTS CAN WE HANDLE?

- Research into relationships shows that ,on average, we can handle about 150 contacts.[3]

- On average, we meet about 200 to 1000[4] new people a year. So our total number of contacts is not limited by our failure to meet new people, but by our brains, which cannot cope with so many relationships.

- It is inherently logical that people with enormous networks have fewer close relationships, while people with limited networks have fewer, but deeper, relationships.

- That is why you should choose your relationships with care. You should be able to handle and maintain your contacts – otherwise they will fade away.

- Do not hesitate to replace contacts in your network. It is natural to set new targets and change approaches to one's challenges – other people do the same.

- However, remember that contacts who do not bring benefits at any given time might still be useful in your network. Anyone can be affected temporarily by unemployment, illness or stress that means they are unable give anything back. Periods like that are times when a contact may need your help the most.

EXERCISE:

1. *Study the map of your network (see tip 7).*

2. *If you have more than 150 close relationships, it is time to decide whether you can handle so many contacts. Do you spend a fair proportion of your time on each of them?*

3. *We often stick with our contacts because we do not have the heart to replace them. However, there should be a fair balance between their relevance to your network, the effort you put into retaining the relationship and the benefits they bring.*

3,4 Dunbar, University of Cambridge. Social cognition on the Internet: Testing constraints on social network size, The Royal Society, 25 June 2012. http://rstb.royalsocietypublishing.org/content/367/1599/2192

12. STRONG AND WEAK CONTACTS

- In research into theoretical networks, the efficiency of networks in providing new qualified and useful contacts has been studied.

- A study by Misner and Steen (2013)[5] concludes that weak contacts, superficial relationships from social media, for example, yield an average of 0.4 new contacts a year, whereas close connections, often face-to-face contacts, yield 7.4 contacts or references a year.

- There is no absolute conclusion concerning the perfect network mix, but the aforementioned study may help you decide how many face-to-face contacts and how many social media contacts will suit your personal challenges.

- Weak connections could have certain advantages: you may benefit from them without having to put much energy into maintaining the contacts; they can offer you surprising opportunities; and they may, over time, become strong relationships if your focus changes.

- Time plays an important role in deciding how close our network relationships will be: the more time we spend with people, the deeper and more stable we consider the relationship.

"THE NETWORKER - CONNECTED MAN - OUTMATCHES THINKING MAN" (UNKNOWN)

EXERCISE:

1. *How many strong and weak contacts do you have in your portfolio? Is this mix balanced to suit your challenges?*

2. *Are there weak contacts you need to upgrade and give higher priority – and strong contacts that should be downgraded?*

[5] Dr Ivan Misner and Director and Partner Max Steén 2013: *The Strength of Strong Ties in Business Referral Networks*, http://globalnetworkingshow.com/quality-v-quantity/

PART Two

OLD-SCHOOL NETWORKING AND THE NEW NETWORKING VERSION 2.0

A WORD
ON OLD-SCHOOL NETWORKING
AND THE NEW NETWORKING
VERSION 2.0

For several years, networking has been a matter of establishing as many contacts as possible, handing out vast numbers of business cards and going to endless meetings.

That exercise cost a lot of time, made our networks complex and erratic and tired out many networkers – especially because they realized that the effort they made was not matched by corresponding gains.

Old-school networking sucks. The point is that there is an easier way and that by doing the exercises in this book you have already generated awareness and concrete data that will support your future networking activities in a more efficient and time-saving way.

This new method is called Networking Version 2.0, and it accounts for the fact that no one is able to maintain hundreds of contacts. We need a manageable and relevant mix of close and loose relationships. However, we have to cut down on the time we spend

on networking – although this should not detract from its overall
positive results.

NETWORKING VERSION 2.0 IS BUILT ON TWO BASIC CONCEPTS:

1. A short-term strategy where you have to define a vision for how
   you want your network to help you out over the next year.

2. A long-term strategy where you have to qualify the networking
   process by identifying and using nodal points.

13. WHAT IS MY VISION? NETWORKING VERSION 2.0

- More often than not, our networking activities – and thus our gains – are decided by pure chance.

- Formulating a clear vision of what you want to achieve via your network gives you visible guidelines that you can follow in a goal-orientated way.

- The world is ever-evolving That is why your vision can only be assumed to be valid a year in advance.

- You can work from a business perspective or a personal perspective – or a mix of both. Alternatively, you can have, for instance, two business perspectives. If you choose to have more than one vision, you should develop a plan for each of them.

• The subjects on which you focus could be education, a new job, setting up business, expanding your business or something very personal you would like to achieve.

EXERCISE:

1. *Use one-to-two hours to describe your most important vision for the following year: what would you like to achieve? For example, if you would like to give your job functions an overhaul, the following questions might be relevant: where are you heading professionally, and what role or kind of business are you going for?*

2. *Your vision should be as concrete as possible. The more concrete, the more operational.*

14. WITH WHAT DO I NEED HELP? NETWORKING VERSION 2.0

- Once your vision has been set out, you have to determine which processes it must go through to succeed.

- What type of competences, knowledge, experience and economic environment do you need, and should there be a specific order?

- Next, focus on your potential challenges: what might you need help with? Which problems would you find it difficult to address on your own?

- The problem areas with which we need help often halt our aspirations and visions. By facing these obstacles, however, you can start breaking down the barriers.

- One phase of this process is having the courage to tell the people around you about your vision and your challenges. The advantage of expressing your vision is that whenever you talk about it, you raise awareness of it and enable your network to come up with possible solutions.

- In certain cases, of course, we are dealing with questions of patents and sensitive subjects that are not suitable for publication.

- Talking about your dreams and visions can be a great door-opener for you. Think how privileged you have felt in the past, when a contact let you in on his or her new venture or passion.

EXERCISE:

1. *When you have ascertained your vision, you should conduct a critical evaluation and identify your challenges. What can you do to achieve your mission, and what do you need help with? Identify your top three most important challenges.*

2. *Tell your closest contacts about your vision.*

3. *If you have not yet defined it, tell them about one of your professional passions.*

4. *After that, consider how your vision was received and how your openness appealed to your contacts.*

15. WHO COULD BE MY HELPERS? NETWORKING VERSION 2.0

- When you have defined where you need help it is time to start using the diagram representing your network. Are there relevant people available?

- Often, contacts cannot be used as a direct source of help. They cannot necessarily get you an appointment with the managing director of your favorite company just like that. They may, however, be able to help you along by discussing your challenges or connecting you with present employees or former colleagues at the workplace, or people from similar companies. Consider this process a part of a research phase that could bring you closer to your goal.

- Never ask for the impossible. Do not ask a contact to get you a job in his or her company. For most people, that demand is simply not realistic, and your enquiry is bound to establish a no-win situation for both of you. Instead, ask about company details so you become more aware of management and decision makers. Show respect and make sure it will be a win-win situation for all parties.

- A very important point to bear in mind: it is not only people with whom you share profiles and generally agree that might prove helpful on your journey. Contacts with oblique approaches can offer eye-openers and offer extremely constructive guidance.

EXERCISE:

It is now time to make your vision concrete. Name the people you think could help you reach your goal.
You must consider:

1. *Relevant people who are already contacts in your network.*

2. *Relevant contacts who can connect you to what you need in order to live out your vision.*

16. LONG-TERM STRATEGY - NODAL POINTS NETWORKING VERSION 2.0

- The long-term strategy is a time-saving shortcut to a workable network.

- Nodal points can be explained by referring to a flight map: if you replace the destinations on the map with a person's network, it is obvious that the contact that replaces Frankfurt, for example, or Nairobi has numerous incoming and outgoing contacts. A contact like that is called a nodal point. This contact reaches out to a great number of contexts and opportunities.

- Small destinations, on the other hand, may have just one route, here interpreted as a person with a very limited network with little immediate access to contacts and opportunities.

- The point of the metaphor is that a nodal point represents a person, an organization or a network with an extremely high concentration of relationships.

- If you have two-to-five nodal points in your network, you are well off as these contacts will reach out and offer much more diversity than your own network.

- Having effective nodal points means that you have to maintain only two-to-five important relationships instead of keeping several hundred contacts alive. But do not forget: this relationship works both ways. You should always be available to your nodal point and be ready to help.

- Networking Version 2.0 does not exclude you from being a member of sundry other networking groups and arrangements. It may even be helpful in detecting new potential nodes. Networking Version 2.0 is a guarantee that your network is operational without spending too much time on it.

EXERCISE:

1. *From now on you should focus attention on potential nodal points. They are everywhere, but to identify them you must be highly attentive and fully aware of your networking needs.*

2. *Nodal points are to be found all over the place: your banker, your accountant, in football clubs and lodges, in your present network, at work and while doing leisure activities.*

PART THREE

INTROVERTS VERSUS EXTROVERTS

A WORD
INTROVERTS VERSUS EXTROVERTS

Most people display features from both personality types – introvert and extrovert – but for many, one of the two character traits is dominant.

We are quick to label people: extroverts talk to anyone and often become the social centre of attention. Introverts are observant, shy and not interested in taking part in social activities. Introverts often maintain a dislike of networking, claiming it is too complicated and demanding; but it does not have to be like that.

It is true that introverts are often reserved and shy, but this personality type also includes qualities that are extremely useful when it comes to networking and establishing relationships.

17. INTROVERTS

- Before you give up the struggle to become an outgoing networker, it is important to know that the introverted characteristic also includes strong networking competences. Many of the world's most successful leaders are introverts by nature and developed their extrovert characteristics later in life.

- As an introvert, you will often be an active and attentive listener who does not feel the need to dominate the conversation. Good listeners are in short supply so your company may be much appreciated.

- Many introverts are able to retain focus during a conversation, and a slightly nerdy way of thinking sometimes challenges others in an inspiring and different way.

- Try pairing yourself with an extrovert and go to meetings and events. Let your partner pave the way for you by attracting attention until you are acclimatized.

- If you have participated in a successful event – a speech or a course – it may seem daunting and chaotic to track down the host or the speaker to ask questions or say thanks. A handwritten card or an email with a response would be an easy and visible alternative follow-up.

- Expand your existing network. Ask someone you know to introduce you to new contacts.

- Use the internet to enter into dialogue with relevant people. Later, when you meet up face-to-face you can use elements from your online communication in your conversation to get it flowing.

EXERCISE:

Do this exercise while you are moving around your town:

1. *Say hello to people you do not know, smile and give the strangers a friendly nod. Say good morning and good evening.*

2. *Try to open a conversation at work, in the supermarket queue or during a leisure activity. People will be a little surprised at first, but most will love it, and you will have taken a big step forward.*

18. EXTROVERTS

• As an extrovert, you are a person who generates energy by being with many people in groups and forums where you are able to express yourself.

• Most extroverts see themselves as great networkers, which indeed they often are, because they have the courage to make contact with people they do not know.

• Be careful not to intimidate other people. Many non-extroverts may feel you are 'too much' and that you are overstepping their limits.

- Take care not to end up as an entertainer instead of a networker. Sometimes, extrovert characteristics may get in the way of your positive qualities and competences. For that very reason, it can be difficult to establish close contacts. Extroverts often have extensive networks, based on many loose relationships.

- It is not necessarily your responsibility to make sure everything works or that conversation flows. Let others talk and stay in the background at times. Be an active listener.

- An active listener focuses on his or her companion's story and does not interrupt. Make supplementary comments to show you are taking information on board and, through body language, demonstrate an interest in the conversation. It takes a great deal of self-restraint at first, but soon you will experience the positive atmosphere that arises when you give other people space and attention.

EXERCISE:

1. *Next time you are in a large group, tell yourself you are not responsible for awkward pauses or poor entertainment. From now on, you have the right to relax and spend time listening and establishing intimacy with your colleagues.*

PART FOUR

BUILDING
RELATIONSHIPS

A WORD
ON BUILDING RELATIONSHIPS

It is wonderful to be selected as a contact by a person who opens the door to vast networking opportunities, but it does not happen very often. That is why you have to be open and enquiring – but certainly not obtrusive. Accept the fact that it takes time to establish loyal and trusting relationships.

When you establish relationships, the 'VCP model' is an effective working tool.[6] It describes the process of creation, growth and strengthening of business, and professional and personal relationships.

The VCP model looks like this: Visibility + Credibility = Profitability

The model shows that the first step is to make yourself VISIBLE. Over time, as people get to know you, you will achieve CREDIBILITY. But not until you have attained credibility will you see PROFITABILITY.

Many people believe that after the first contact it is possible to go straight to profitability and exploit the potential of the recently-acquired relationship, but that is almost always an incorrect assumption.

If you find it difficult to transform new relationships into good contacts it might be because you do not allow the first two levels of the model the time needed to build strong relationships.

The next two tips present visibility and credibility as effective working tools.

[6]VCP model created by Dr. Ivan Misner

19. VISIBILITY

- Visibility means that the people around you should be able to decode who you are and what you can do in a relatively short space of time.

- It is very important that, through your visibility, you display the person you want to be and the competences you want to represent. Visibility is your shop window display.

- Visibility can be established in a number of ways and locations. It is all about you and the way you navigate and present yourself.

- It is also about visibility on your website and social media platforms, in the media, via PR and marketing, your business cards and videos.

- Always remember: you are responsible for the message your recipients gain about you.

- Make it easy for recipients to understand and relate to you and your message. Communicate in a simple, non-kaleidoscopic way.

- Visibility is very much about the way you present yourself. Complex titles and long CVs do not work. In contrast, good narratives and metaphors do.

- A business card is a nice thing to hand out to people when you are on the road. Including a photo on this will enhance recognition and the likelihood that you will be remembered.

EXERCISE:

1. *What would you like people to say about you?*
   Find two essential messages.

2. *Ask three of your contacts what they thought about you*
   when they first met you. Is this the message you want
   to convey?

20. CREDIBILITY

- Once, through your visibility, you have piqued people's interest in you as a person, your services or your products, the next step is to boost your credibility in the relationship.

- It takes time to build good relationships. Best practice in terms of the transition from visibility to credibility is to find ways to help or add value for your new potential contact. We all love people who help us develop our competences and add prestige to our business.

- There are many ways to show a would-be contact that you are giving him or her priority over others in your network. Invite the potential contact to meetings, be an active listener (see tip 28), introduce the person to other potential relations (see tip 39), share relevant knowledge and offer your assistance at all levels.

- Credibility goes both ways, of course. You need to have a positive gut feeling that the contact-to-be has the ability and the will to add value for you as well.

- If the credibility phase proceeds successfully, you will gradually move on to profitability, and the exchange of services, knowledge and confidentiality is likely to become a natural part of your relationship.

EXERCISE:

1. *Select two people with whom you would like to network and establish a relationship.*

2. *Apply the VCP model and allow the time needed to get through all phases.*

21. YOUR PERSONAL VALUE

- When you are networking and working with the VCP model, it is important that you are aware of your value and capabilities. How can you make yourself visible, and what are you able to share with your contacts?

- Few people have a realistic understanding of their own value, which is disastrous because that is what makes you unique and attractive. It is an overlooked aspect of building your personal image and brand as a competent networker.

- If you want to estimate your own value in relation to your network, you can make your assessment according to the following:
  1. Your personality
  2. Your professionalism
  3. Your experience
  4. Your network

A simple way to make your value concrete is to ask the following question: "What encourages people to contact me, to communicate with me and to benefit from me?"

1. Your personality. Are you good at motivating people, listening, challenging and implementing new initiatives?
2. Your professionalism. Do you have specialized knowledge within your field of work?
3. Your career experience. Do you have experience that is special and unique? Do you have a passion?
4. Your network. Is it of great potential value to others? Are there members of your network to whom other people might like to be introduced? Remember that a good network is an attractive commodity.

EXERCISE:

1. *Go through the four parameters and write down at least two responses against each. You are likely to note values you would never before have considered effective networking commodities.*

2. *Ask recently established contacts whether they see you as a valuable relationship, and why.*

3. *In exchange, tell them how they contribute for you and to your network. This conversation opener often results in a more constructive and meaningful dialogue and a further development of your relationship.*

PART FIVE

COMMUNICATION

A WORD
ON COMMUNICATION

How do we communicate when we want to establish contact with another person or we want to sell something?

The classic mistake is that we start talking a lot about ourselves and our products and services. We go, as it were, into salesman mode. Funnily enough, most of us feel uncomfortable about it – but we do it anyway.

If you want to establish a good relationship, it is crucial that the focus of attention should be on your conversational partner. Focus should be shifted from *"how can you help me?"* to *"how can I help you?"*

When you give the other person your full attention and show that you are interested in them, the creation of a positive atmosphere is already well under way, and that is a good starting point for establishing a useful relationship.

To create a positive atmosphere, you will need to be able to handle a number of communicative disciplines such as questioning techniques, small talk and active listening.

A good role model who masters these disciplines is world-famous TV host Oprah Winfrey, who, in her talk shows, addresses both serious and amusing subjects.

Oprah is able to establish a very positive atmosphere. She shows openness, empathy and intimacy, and to top it all, she is a fabulous listener. Through her questions and attitude, it is obvious to her audience that she has real presence. She is encouraging, but also sharp with her guests.

An American reporter once said, "Oprah made a fortune being an active listener".

At the same time, she is living proof that giving other people attention does not detract from one's own opportunities; she has set up a fantastic platform for sharing her personal opinions and boosting her earnings.

REMEMBER TO CREATE A POSITIVE ATTITUDE AND TO COMMUNICATE WITH YOUR CONVERSATION PARTNER'S INTERESTS IN MIND. IT PAYS OFF; THE OPPOSITE WILL BE A WASTE OF TIME FOR BOTH OF YOU.

22. QUESTIONING SKILLS AND TECHNIQUES

- When you initiate a conversation with another person, small talk is the platform that allows you to prepare, mentally, for the essential part of the conversation. (see tip 26).

- From a communication perspective, open questions are useful to get conversation flowing as they often result in slightly longer answers and cannot be answered with a simple "yes" or "no".

- Open questions typically begin with wh-words:
  What do you expect to get out of this meeting?
  Why did you join group two?

- In addition to open questions, there are closed questions, which are typically answered with a "yes" or a "no":
  Are you going to the meeting tomorrow?
  Do you know any of the managers?
  These are questions that do not necessarily help move a conversation on.

- Wh-questions are super-efficient conversation starters, but stop using them strategically as soon as you get talking. If you continue, your talk may be seen as an interrogation or a journalistic interview. The goal is to develop a relaxed conversation in which you participate equally.

- Keep up-to-date on news, films, social issues, theatre and books. Insight into these fields will enable you to start or join a conversation anytime and feel at ease throughout the entire discussion.

- A good questioning technique should be matched by an efficient listening technique (see tip 28). Quite often, your conversation partner's answer will sow the seeds of the next relevant question you may ask.

EXERCISE:

Next time you meet a new, relevant contact, think of a strategy via which to structure your conversation by means of questions:

1. *Start by using small talk*

2. *Focus on your partner and make him or her feel at ease*

3. *Use wh-words to collect information*

You now have a platform from which to kick-start your conversation.

23. BE AWARE OF YOUR BRANDING PROFILE

- It is very important to be aware of your brand – no matter whether you have a job or are looking for a job, are an entrepreneur or run a business.

- Having a brand means having a product label for yourself, your product or your services. A clear and informative brand makes it easier for other people to respond to you and your wishes.

- Creating a brand can be a very constructive personal process as we are seldom fully aware of our strengths and the precise purpose of establishing contacts in a network.

- The questions below will help you clarify how you, as a networker, can present yourself and your project or business in the best possible way.

- What are the characteristics of you and your product?
    1. Who are you and what are your product's selling points?
    2. What do other people think of you and your product?
    3. Who knows you and your product?
    4. How can you and your product make a difference to other people?

EXERCISE:

1. *Go through the questions on your own. Discuss your answers with a person or a group that knows you or your business. Maybe they will see details of which you were not aware.*

2. *Summarize the results. This should enable you to define, and give words to, your brand.*

24. SIMPLE COMMUNICATION

- Quite often you come across people with exotic titles and 'special competences'. If you ask what they stand for, you often get a disappointing answer.

- Many people believe that kaleidoscopic and complex communication has an edge over everyday language and that professional language signals intelligence and establishes respect. However, that is not the case in networking, quite the opposite.

- The brain has great difficulty remembering something it does not understand. It remembers images and stories, but facts and incomprehensible information are difficult to retain.

- Networking is about knowledge sharing and supporting one another so you have to able to understand and remember what you are told. That is why it is critical to communicate in a simple way, and preferably in terms of images and metaphors.

- Another reason to focus on simple communication skills is that, hopefully, our messages will be spread by a number of different people and networks.

- If your message is to be shared, it is essential that:
    1. The readers understand the message.
    2. The message is so simple and easy to summarize that its original form is retained as it is communicated by different people.

SIMPLICITY IS THE KEYWORD IF YOU AND YOUR MESSAGES ARE TO BE REMEMBERED. USE IMAGES, METAPHORS AND STORIES. THE SIMPLER YOUR COMMUNICATION IS, THE MORE LIKELY YOU ARE TO GET YOUR MESSAGE THROUGH THE NETWORK IN ITS ORIGINAL FORM.

EXERCISE:

If you communicate with people within your own area of business, professional language is absolutely acceptable. But if you tell ordinary people about your job, how do you express yourself?

1. *Give an account of your job so that:*

- *A bank employee understands and is interested in your work*

- *A politician understands and is interested in your work*

- *A hair stylist understands and is interested in your work*

2. *Remember to use metaphors, stories and images in your account so that you make it easier for listeners to comprehend. For example, a computer expert once described his role in this way: "I deal with the brain and heart of your computer."*

25. SHOW CURIOSITY

- Many people are not particularly curious or observant about their surroundings.

- It is a rare luxury to meet an observant listener who asks relevant, stimulating and interesting questions and generally seems to be interested in you and your business.

- Showing interest in other people is the best way to make new contacts. You could develop into such a person, and you would soon become a much-coveted partner – because networkers like that are few and far between.

- If you run into popular networkers, you will notice that they seldom talk about themselves; they listen, ask questions and show genuine curiosity. On the other hand, they are very good at moving on if they find the conversation superficial. This is often done in a very elegant way so that their conversation partner barely notices he or she has been left alone.

EXERCISE:

1. *Practise using wh-questions to show curiosity and genuine interest. Ask about the other person's challenges and experiences.*

2. *Ask at least three questions before you detail your own knowledge and experience.*

3. *Be curious in your everyday life and practise asking questions before you comment or give your opinion.*

26. THE ANATOMY OF SMALL TALK

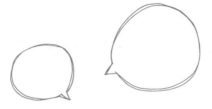

- Small talk is polite conversation without any important content. It is an excellent means of getting to know other networkers.

- It is during the small talk phase that we decode one another's views, attitudes and status and decide whether to continue with our chat or not.

- You have to keep the chat going and in this process determine whether rapport can be established. If this happens, it is possible to move on to a more content-orientated conversation. If one of the parties is not interested, it is possible to withdraw without suffering any major embarrassment.

- Small talk also paves the way for establishing a good atmosphere. For example, when you ask about a person's health, compliment somebody on their clothing or achievements or open a dialogue about "spring being just around the corner".

- Many people wrongly believe that the first few minutes of a chat are critical if you want to project yourself as being an intelligent person. However, small talk is about establishing equal status between participants in order to create a sense of security and balance in the relationship so that both parties want to continue the conversation.

- When we engage in small talk, the focus should be on what we have in common rather than what sets us apart. That is why it is unwise to bring up religious, political or value-based subjects in this initial phase.

- Here are some useful and harmless topics you could use during the small talk phase: a recent meeting or business event, the weather, films and books, newspaper headlines.

EXERCISE:

1. *Make a habit of talking to people you do not know at the bus stop, in the supermarket or in restaurants and cafes.*

2. *Practise being the one who initiates small talk. Use wh-questions. Preferably, say something meaningful about yourself so that your conversation partner can continue the chat.*

3. *If you are afraid of making small talk, you should prepare two or three questions before entering the room. This will settle your nerves if your mind suddenly goes blank.*

27. PARALLEL CONVERSATIONS

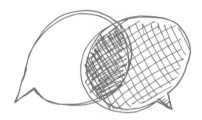

- Do you recognize the following scenario? You have just returned from a fantastic holiday, and you have a lot to report. You start talking about the wild animals you got close to. As soon as you have finished the first sentence, however, your conversation partner takes over and starts talking about his trip to Kenya. After that, the conversation fluctuates between Kenya and your holiday, with both parties trying to continue their stories.

- These are parallel conversations: a form of conversation where one story gives inspiration to the other.

- The problem with that way of communicating is that you never really get to the heart of the matter and never unfurl the potential of either story.

- It is a privilege to be allowed to talk about your experiences, wishes and frustrations. If that is accompanied by a conversation partner who listens actively, asks good questions and is capable of developing your story and putting it into context, you will feel fortunate to be talking to them.

• Maybe, over time, you could turn yourself into such a gift to your contacts. You would be liked for it and become an attractive conversation partner in your network.

EXERCISE:

Parallel storytelling is an integral part of everyday communication, and you should make a great effort not to fall into that conversational pitfall.

1. *Approach one of your regular conversation partners and explain how parallel conversations work and their consequences. Find a subject in which he is interested. Give him five minutes to express his views on the subject. During the five-minute period, your only task is to listen, ask questions and encourage him to expand on his story. In short, stay in his narrative and do not initiate one of your own.*

2. *After five minutes, switch roles!*

It is a difficult, but very rewarding, exercise that can help you become a future master networker.

28. BE AN ACTIVE LISTENER

- Communication is a two-way process of talking and listening. One might think listening is an easy task, but unfortunately, it is a very demanding job. Being an ideal listener requires you to be fully present, with mind and body.

- There are five different listening techniques:
  1. Selective listening: you choose to hear what you feel like hearing and shut out unwanted information.
  2. External listening: you do not hear anything and do not respond to what is being said.
  3. Internal listening: what you hear is processed and interpreted through your personal filter, which is based on personal experience.

4. Focused listening: here you are fully present and focused. You perceive your conversation partner's needs and wishes and ask questions from his or her perspective.
5. Intuitive listening: focused listening has now become an integral and natural part of the conversation.

- Most people will recognize at least one of the first three positions. We seldom come across a person who combines positions four and five – although it is a fantastic experience when it happens. Optimal focused listening includes corresponding posture in which eye contact plays a crucial role. People who are focused or intuitive listeners are often successful sounding boards and networkers.

EXERCISE:

1. *Which of the five listening positions do you generally adopt?*

2. *In your opinion, is that position a helpful one for you?*

3. *If you are not a focused listener, how can you intensify your listening next time you are having an important conversation?*

29. SUM UP MEETINGS AND GIVE POSITIVE FEEDBACK

- When you have become an experienced networker, you could show your surplus energy by summing up your meeting. What have we been talking about, what were our conclusions, and how do we move on from here?

- Explain what you got out of the meeting and what you will be looking forward to when you meet again. Agree on a date for a follow-up meeting.

- Everyone loves to receive praise, so tell your contacts what they are good at. It could be their performance at a meeting or the way they tackle challenges – in their career as well as in their private life.

- Only commend people's efforts when you mean it, though, and give reasons for your praise. Giving people credit where it is due often establishes a special atmosphere. It is a well-known fact that praising and being praised cause dopamine to be released.[6]

- Praise creates a win-win experience for both parties and thus a closer relationship.

EXERCISE:

1. *Praising and receiving praise can be quite difficult.*

2. *Practise praising your contacts. Next time you see a person doing something good, give praise and give your reasons for it.*

3. *Receiving praise can also be a challenge. Do not be embarrassed, and do not bat it away. Say, "thanks, I'm glad to hear that!"*

[6] Dopamine is a neurotransmitter that helps control the brains reward and pleasure centres.

30. WHEN YOU CANNOT STOP PEOPLE TALKING

- When you begin activating our networking tips and become an attractive networker, you are also going to attract people with a great need to talk. It is the price you have to pay and a problem you have to tackle.

- Lots of people have a great need to talk, probably because the world is short of ears that are willing to listen.

- When you run into interesting, but very talkative people, it is up to you to decide whether they are potential contacts worth pursuing – or a drain on your time.

- If you think they may be a useful contact, you could arrange a meeting at a future date when you have more time to carry on your conversation in more relaxed circumstances.

- If you cannot decide whether they are a useful contact or not, there is only one way out. During a natural pause in conversation, ask the person if he or she would like to hear about your business. It is a bit rude to ask a direct question in such a way, but it gives you a quick clarification. Do they have contact potential or is he or she so self-centred that a positive dialogue is not an option? If he or she is the latter type of person, say, "thanks for your time and interest" and move on. Always remember to say thanks.

EXERCISE:

1. *Assess how you behave when talking to other people. What is your listening-to-talking ratio? Do you make room for your conversation partners?*

2. *Are you aware of the signals people send - do you give contacts space to contribute to your dialogue?*

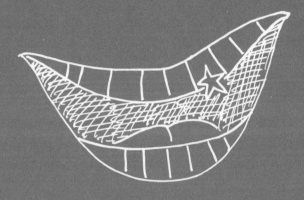

PART SIX

APPEAL AND ATTITUDE

A WORD
ON APPEAL AND ATTITUDE

How do you meet new people? Funny question, but then again, maybe it isn't. It may be a decisive factor in determining the success of your project.

Our non-verbal communication has more impact than we think, and that is a bit scary as we often attach utmost importance to our words when we introduce ourselves or are speaking to other people.

At worst, our communication may prove a total waste of time because our body language and tone of voice, the factors we forget to take into account, distract people's attention so that they do not get the intended message.

It is not only when we meet new people that non-verbal communication speaks volumes. When we have a conversation, even with someone we know well, words convey less than a third of the message; two-thirds is conveyed through non-verbal elements.[8]

The body is a tell-tale, and it is difficult to control. It is fairly easy to tell a lie but much more difficult to make your body do the same in a convincing manner.

Non-verbal language sends a lot of information to other people and we are undoubtedly judged according to the overall impression we make.

"WHEN PEOPLE ARE NERVOUS THEY SPEAK FASTER. DO THE OPPOSITE, SLOW DOWN AND PAUSE AND YOUR AUDIENCE WILL BE ON AGAIN." (VICTOR BORGE)

[a] Ray Birdwhistell, 1970 Kinesics and Context: pp. 86-87. University of Pennsylvania.

31. BUILD YOURSELF UP

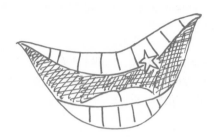

- We all know the feeling of having a bad day. It is a tough job to stand up straight and look people in the eye, and it feels more natural to retreat into oneself. The first thing we register when we decode body language is people's posture so if you want to signal a surplus of mental resources, it is critical to stand up straight and have the courage to make eye contact. Otherwise, you give yourself away.

- If you doubt yourself, others will doubt you as well. That is why you have to work on your self-confidence. The easiest way to do that is to give other people your attention. Ask questions and give praise. People who take a genuine interest in others and praise them, are attractive, and it is going to boost your self-esteem to feel that people like you.

- Stop telling yourself what you cannot do. Instead, make long lists of things you can do for other people.

- Making good eye contact suggests openness, honesty, energy and responsiveness. People who send these types of signals are considered strong. If you have not got the courage to look people in the eye, it is hard work to get on the same wavelength. So it is important to practise and to find the courage to do it.

- A smile is at the heart of building rapport in many cultures and generates positive reactions and responsiveness. According to psychologist Paul Ekman[9], we activate the autonomic nervous system when we smile, which releases endorphins in the body and makes us feel comfortable. At the same time, we seem to become likeable to other people.[10]

"PEOPLE WILL FORGET WHAT YOU SAID, BUT PEOPLE WILL NEVER FORGET HOW YOU MADE THEM FEEL." MAYA ANGELOU

EXERCISE:

1. *If you are falling down a hole, never think:*

- *I just don't understand this*

- *I'm no good at this*

- *I haven't got any energy for this*

2. *Eliminate your negative thoughts: return to your notes from tip 21 and remind yourself of all the skills that make you valuable.*

[9] Paul Ekman, psychologist, the world's leading expert on facial expressions.
[10] Paul Ekman, 2013: How Smiles Control Us All: http://www.theatlantic.com/health/archive/2013/01/how-smiles-control-us-all/272588/

32. BE A LIKEABLE AND A "GO-TO" PERSON

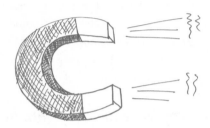

- No one wants to approach people who radiate negative energy. We are almost afraid it is contagious.

- People with a positive attitude are often master networkers and function like magnets.

- A magnetic persona, or a go-to person, emanates passion, positivity, credibility and self-confidence, and pays attention to other people.

- The most important goal in networking is to make the people around you accept and like you and you must also understand the rules of the game. You are not supposed to be an actor; on the contrary, you have to be yourself and be self-contained. That is easier said than done. The trick is to strike a balance between being adaptable and available and retaining your personality and individual characteristics.

- Give your honest opinion – with responsibility. You attract people because you are honest, but formulate criticism in a constructive and positive way. Help your contacts on their way, do not hinder them.

- Attentiveness is a key element of networking. So it is a really bad habit to let your eyes wander around the room when talking to somebody. Stop it! You are only undermining yourself.

- For many leaders, it is necessary to be the person around whom others gather. The problem is that it takes a lot of energy and is a struggle for many people to maintain.

- Use your personality to attract others to you. It is not, however, enough to attract attention. Others should feel there is a genuine incentive to seek you out. In this book there are lots of tips about how to attract others to you. Focus especially on being present, being an active listener, being balanced, communicating in a simple way and maintaining good relationships.

PEOPLE TAKE AN INTEREST IN PEOPLE WHO ARE INTERESTED IN THEM!

EXERCISE:

1. *If a good friend was asked to give your eulogy, what would you like them to say?*

33. TESTOSTERONE VERSUS CORTISOL

- Non-verbal communication sends a lot of information to those around us, and there is no doubt that we are judged according to a range of factors.

- Scientists have been unanimously agreed for many years that, via the brain, we can control our body language so that we achieve conscious ways of acting.

- The new discovery is that a reversible process exists in that body language can influence the chemical balance of the brain, resulting in very useful opportunities. Professor Amy Cuddy[11] has, through a research project, revealed new insights into human interaction.[12] Her experiment investigates the balance between the male sex hormone testosterone and the stress hormone cortisol when the body is exposed to 'high power' and 'low power' body language. The experiment was based on an observation that people with a lot of energy, such as great speakers, have a very high level of testosterone when they are on stage, while at the same time, the level of cortisol in their brain is low.

- The research paper concluded that adopting confident body language can increase testosterone levels in the brain and provide a perceptible feeling of energy and power. Simultaneously, levels of stress and anxiety are curbed, which further strengthens the impression of strength and confidence.

- You increase your testosterone level by adopting high power body language for just a few minutes.

EXERCISE:

1. *Find a quiet place where you can concentrate on this exercise. Seated or standing, adopt one or more of the high-power poses for two minutes.*

2. *Feel the difference – a feeling of energy and power flowing through your body. This technique can be used when you go to networking meetings, job interviews or drinks receptions.*

[11] Amy Cuddy, associated professor Harvard Business School.
[12] http://www.hbs.edu/faculty/Pages/profile.aspx?facId=491042

34. SHAKING HANDS

- There are many ways to initiate a business relationship. The way we do it is highly dependent on culture, nationality and context.

- Common greetings range from verbal expressions to hand signals to a kiss on the cheek. In Europe, many people use the physical handshake, but we often forget that we decode and assess one another by the handshakes we give and receive. When we shake hands enthusiastically, we forget that we are transmitting important data about ourselves.

- A limp or a firm handshake immediately conveys information about us as a communicator.

- What happens if your handshake does not transmit the signals you wish it to and tells a different story than intended about your personality, brand or status? There are two possible scenarios: either you are considered to be a different type of person to the one you are trying to present, or you trigger a lot of confusion in the recipient of the handshake.

- That is why it is important to be aware of the style of your handshake. Handshakes can be graded on a scale of one to 10.

1------------------------------------5------------------------------------10

very limp   extremely firm

- It is critical to know the style of your handshake so that you avoid the limp handshake and the ultra-firm version. The ideal is to get as close to a five as possible.

- It is possible to improve your handshake. In principle, you should go for a five, from the receiver's point of view. If it is a woman who is slight of build, your handshake should probably be at the soft end of the middle range, while a sturdy man could be greeted in a firmer manner. Generally, take care to tailor your handshake to your conversation partner so that he or she feels seen and understood. If this moment goes well, there is a fair chance that your further communication will be successful.

- A handshake should always be accompanied by eye contact and a warm smile.

EXERCISE:

1. *It is a great idea to practise with friends and colleagues. Shake hands and comment on what you experience.*

2. *Swap roles and let your partner do the same. An example: you receive a handshake which is too limp, and you tell your partner it is a three and to squeeze a little harder.*

3. *Continue until you receive an optimal handshake. This exercise is likely to create a good atmosphere and a lot of laughter. Both parties become aware of their handshakes and learn to send signals that are more conscious.*

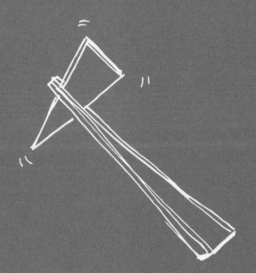

PART SEVEN

TECHNICAL SKILLS

A WORD
ON TECHNICAL SKILLS

It is one thing to be aware that a relevant network of contacts is necessary for a successful career, but another thing to develop and implement the networking competences that make it pay off.

- It can be difficult to find a technique that makes it a pleasure to enter a room with lots of unknown people.
- It can be a challenge to learn how to exploit your networking resources optimally.
- It can be challenging to acquire the skills to build networks and make contacts.

This chapter deals with concrete techniques that will help you exploit and develop your potential as a networker and make you a valuable resource for your network.

35. GROUP SKILLS

- We all know how comfortable it feels to be attending a meeting with a group of friendly colleagues. It is a cosy place, you feel self-assured and do not have to look around for allies or pretend to be busy or on-the-ball.

- It is natural and logical to connect with people who are similar to oneself. In groups, we find security and feel accepted and understood.

- The problem is that if you only connect with colleagues and friends, you are likely to miss out on inspiration and different types of relationships:
  - Relationships that could broaden your horizons by challenging deeply ingrained attitudes and behaviours

- Relationships that could lead to new and different contacts, assistance and maybe optimize and future-proof your networks

• Search for contacts and networks different from yourself, and reach upwards into the hierarchy. If you want to become good at something, look for an expert in the field. If you want to learn writing skills, identify a good communicator. If you want to make money, search for a rich entrepreneur. Profit by the success of people who are at the cutting edge of what they do.

EXERCISE:

1. Next time you attend a meeting, force yourself to leave the people you know well. If things should get too challenging, you can always return.

2. Another option is to start making small talk with a total stranger at the buffet or the hot drinks machine and see what comes out of it.

36. ENTERING AN UNKNOWN ROOM

- A potential nightmare lurks behind the door, when you enter a room filled with strangers. Even though you may have done it plenty of times in the past, you may still feel nervous and insecure.

- It is difficult because, first of all, you are 'read' and assessed by everyone else in the room, and second, you have to make quite a few decisions in a very short space of time.

- More often than not, you do not know what to expect: the layout or décor of the room; where the food, drinks or toilets are situated. Nor do you know who is in the room – whether you will find familiar faces in the crowd or be left to fend for yourself.

- Amid fear and doubt, you have to make a quick decision about where you are heading in the room, and most people are hugely relieved when they spot acquaintances. Or even better, when these acquaintances beckon them over. You are saved embarrassment and your heart will stop beating so fast.

"I'VE HAD A LOT OF WORRIES IN MY LIFE, MOST OF WHICH HAVE NEVER HAPPENED." MARK TWAIN

EXERCISE:

1. *The first thing you can do to overcome your fears is to realize that many of the guests in the room feel exactly like you. Some are just better at hiding it.*

2. *Try to imagine the situation before you enter the room. Visualize what you expect to see and who you are going to meet. Prepare two or three small talk questions so that you have the energy to chat with people you meet on your way.*

3. *Put forward the best version of yourself. Adopt an agreeable manner and show you have been looking forward to participating and feel comfortable in other people's company.*

4. *If there are people you know in the crowd, join them and feel how you calm down. When you feel calm again, move on. Old friends and business contacts can always be reached, but right now you should be on the look-out for new potential contacts.*

37. WHO IS OPEN TO BEING APPROACHED?

- Because we feel anxious in large crowds, we often stick with people we know, even though we are aware that it would be desirable to mix things up a bit. We are passive and wait for others to approach us. Unfortunately, this seldom happens, or we are approached by the wrong people.

- Instead of waiting, be proactive yourself. Approach an interesting person, start making small talk, or if it is a group of people, ask them if you can join them. We always expect to be rejected, but it seldom happens. If you were standing alone, wouldn't you be grateful if somebody searched you out?

- The best way to show others that you are open to talking to them is by smiling and seeking eye contact.

-

- If you spot people who are on their own, join them. They may be alone for a number of reasons: perhaps they are poor communicators, perhaps they are just insecure and waiting for a pleasant person to join them or they could be a 'person in transfer', who has just left a group or picked up food and is now looking for new people to talk to.

- If you spot two people standing side-by-side, it might be a signal that they wish to go their separate ways, but are anxious about being left standing on their own or about leaving the other person alone. So they are waiting for someone to do something. You could be the person who goes over to them and starts making small talk. Perhaps all three of you could have a chat or you could join one of them and enable the other to say "thanks" and move on.

- Finally, there tend to be groups of two or more people standing facing one another and almost forming a circle. This type of group can be difficult to penetrate. Their body language shows they are happy as they are and do not want to be interrupted.

EXERCISE:

Set yourself the ultimate task next time you are in a large crowd:

1. *Select an interesting person and join him or her.*

2. *Decide when it is time to approach the person.*

3. *Take great care to say "thanks" to your current conversation partner at the right time so that you leave the best possible impression of yourself. Remember to be the best version of yourself at all times.*

38. CIRCULATING TECHNIQUES

- Being able to circulate is an integral part of networking. This technique is about achieving your goals when you meet potential contacts face-to-face at large gatherings:

  1. Find a conversation partner – it is ok to start with someone you know to settle your nerves.

  2. After that, seek out the people you have planned to meet. If you have not planned anything, approach people who look interesting (see tip 37).

  3. Walk over to your first contact. Establish a good rapport and chat for five to 10 minutes. If you want to continue your conversation, arrange a further meeting. There is no need to spend precious networking time on a conversation that could be better carried on at a later date. Make an appointment, fix a date and time when you will meet or speak over the phone. - If you are the one to follow up on the meeting, do something concrete: provide a cup of coffee or lunch, a relevant contact

or a proposal. It makes it easier for your contact to relate to the appointment. Ideally, a new meeting or telephone call should take place no later than eight days after the first contact has been made.

4. After that, circulate again, find a new conversation partner and repeat the process.

5. Remember not only to focus on your pre-planned contacts, also be open to meeting others who might show an interest in you.

6. Inevitably, you will speak to some people whose potential you fail to see, and you are keen to slope off after a few seconds. Never forget to say "thanks for the chat" before moving on. Maybe your conversation partner will recommend you to one of his or her network contacts.

EXERCISE:

1. *At the next networking session, approach at least three people.*

2. *Talk for five to 10 minutes to each of them.*

3. *Use circulating techniques.*

4. *If you manage to arrange three meetings, remember to celebrate.*

39. INTRODUCTION TECHNIQUES

- It can be hard work having to approach and introduce yourself to a new contact. It is much more comfortable and smooth if you can get one of your existing contacts to introduce you.

- The advantage of being introduced is that you are pre-approved, as it were, and an introduction often includes a few hints as to how the communication can be continued.

- When you introduce contacts to one another, it is important to give them a little information about each other. Highlight common fields of interest, or give a few hints about special competences. Names and job titles do not provide a lot of scope for continuing a conversation.

- As a rule, there is a mutual understanding that "tonight I am going to introduce an interesting person to you, and I expect you to introduce a relevant person to me some other time".

- So remember to introduce people to others and let others introduce their contacts to you. If it does not happen automatically, ask a contact to do you that favour.

- Invite people into your group. It is very uncomfortable to be on your own in a big crowd and to have to interrupt a group of strangers to push your way in. You can make a great difference by introducing or inviting a person into your group. Establishing contact, helping a person into the fold, shows you are confident and empathetic.

EXERCISE:

1. *Invite a useful contact in your network to one of your networking sessions.*

2. *Introduce him or her to the business people you know. If you do somebody a favour they will probably return it in future; at the same time, you get to practise introducing people so that it becomes a natural part of your networking image.*

40. FIND ROLE MODELS

- Even though you are bombarded with tips and guidelines on how to become a successful networker, it can be very difficult to put all this good advice into practice and to start a networking career. For those who already practise the discipline it can be a challenge to implement the advice to improve their skills and create more value.

- Here is a tip that can get you started on networking or improve your daily routine. The keyword is imitation.

- Find a role model who seems to function optimally in a networking context. Analyze this person's strategies, approaches and tricks.

- Find out what appeals about, or what you admire in, the networker's technique. Is it the way he or she approaches other people or the way they position themselves physically? Is it their body language and expression, voice, turn of phrase, or the intensity of their presence? Are they a good listener and do they hold back from talking all the time?

- The next step is to find out how he or she manages to come across as an ideal networker.

- The final task is to adopt what you admire and implement it in your own universe. It takes a lot of practice but it is fun to do and you learn fast this way.

EXERCISE:

1. *Start the process by choosing a role model whose appeal you would like to decode.*

2. *Go to a meeting they are attending. You do not have to contact the person on this occasion, just register what he or she is doing.*

3. *Next, try to contact him or her and have a chat about a subject in which you are both interested. Tell your role model what you admire about his or her networking technique; it is likely to be well received.*

41. STRIKE GOLD

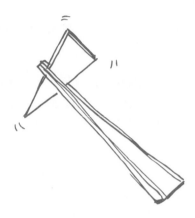

- We tend to associate with people we feel are similar to ourselves. This is only natural because it guarantees acceptance and understanding. But sometimes it is of great value to be offered new challenges.

- Search for networks and network contacts that are different from you. Sometimes it is a good idea to move up the hierarchy. If you want to be wise, look for wise people. If you want to be rich, look for rich people. If you want to be a great business person, look for great business people.

- People who are at the cutting edge of what they do have gained knowledge and experience from which the rest of us can benefit. That will prevent lots of unnecessary mistakes.

- If you want to join a business in which people earn a lot of money, it could be helpful to have an insight into this environment so that you know what to expect should you end up there yourself.

- In other words, court the best people so that your network is in place when you achieve your goals.

- It is often much easier than you would expect to get to know so-called inaccessible people. Contact them. There is nothing to lose by trying. At worst, you will fail to land the contact.

IF YOU WANT TO BE RICH, MOVE TO THE CENTRE OF WEALTH. IF YOU WANT POWER AND INFLUENCE, MAKE YOURSELF VISIBLE AT THE CENTRE OF POWER.

EXERCISE:

1. *Who are your heroes, in relation to your goals? Find two "inaccessible" people in your town or region.*

2. *How do you plan to contact them?*

42. CREATING VALUE THROUGH SOCIAL INDEBTEDNESS

- You gain power and influence when you add value for other people. People tend to repay good deeds, and when they feel kindly treated and are grateful that you helped them, they will be happy to share their own knowledge and assistance.

- Basically, networking is a number of exchanges of services and the most precious insurance in your business and private life. It is based on a principle called "social indebtedness".

- Social indebtedness is at play when we upgrade each other's possibilities and potential.

- You can share lots of things with your contacts, in fact anything and everything:
    - Your knowledge and expertise, which means they can obtain benefits and expand their horizons, in business or in their private lives

- Your own contacts, who can help others achieve their goals and visions
  - Gifts that will enrich your beneficiaries
  - Your services as a sounding board or sparring partner with whom your contacts can have friendly arguments concerning projects and idea development

- Social indebtedness may sound a bit cynical, but it is actually a basic mechanism in our DNA – a kind of survival instinct. What characterizes a skilled networker is that he or she is aware of this function and makes use of it in a constructive and careful way.

- Remember: a principle of, and a precondition for, effective and agreeable networking is that you give before you take.

EXERCISE:

1. *Think of a person to whom you would like to give greater priority in your network. What kind of value could you add for this person? Decide on two things and get started as soon as possible.*

2. *Make a catalogue of services you could offer in future relationships.*

43. EVALUATION

- Networks are organic entities that should be in motion all the time. For that reason, you ought to evaluate your network on a regular basis.

- We tend to build complex networks that easily become chaotic because we include too many casual relationships that are not useful. Too many contacts stop us from recognizing who is really making a difference for us and should be cultivated the most.

- Take regular stock of your network. Have you achieved the goals you set for yourself, or are you wasting your time on contacts and meetings that do not really generate development and value for you?

- Have you found a satisfactory way of handling your talent? Are you developing your ideas, competences and knowledge? Are there people in your network who inspire you, help you and challenge you?

- Do you show your most appealing qualities? Do people know about your passion?

- Are you creating value for the right people? Are your most important contacts receiving the best from you?

EXERCISE:

1. *Look at your networking groups: what do you gain, and how do you contribute?*

2. *Do you act out your passions and do your partners profit from your competences?*

3. *Have you got the right networks, or has it become a habit just to turn up at networking events?*

4. *It is time to take stock!*

PART EIGHT

EXPANSION

A WORD
ON EXPANSION

If you want to be an effective networker, a number of practical tools should be included in your networking kitbag.

For instance, you should always have business cards with you, detailing who you are and the brand you represent. You should also have an "elevator pitch" ready that can be given at short notice.

Being a professional networker, your work life will never be at a standstill. Networks and networking are forever changing, and it is necessary to be open to possibilities and general developments in the field.

Traditional networking – meeting on a regular basis in permanent groups – is nowhere near adequate today. It is much more up to each individual to design goals, reach out to new contacts and act decisively. Being a member of a few established networks does not ensure that you gain the optimal benefits from the time and resources you invest in the meetings.

If you want to work professionally and effectively, it is critical to be active and open to new opportunities, to continue being visible and accommodating and to stand out from the crowd.

44. INFORMATIONAL INTERVIEWS

- Many people discover the value of networking when they want a career change or are stuck in their job-hunting process. In that situation it is, of course, very important to communicate your wishes throughout your network, but an alternative solution could be to make use of informational interviews.

- The standard operating procedure is to send off a job application form and wait for an answer. Generally, the success rate for this is shockingly low. So why not do something very different?

- The informational interview is a tool that involves contacting and having a meeting with an experienced business person who works in the field into which you would like to enter. It is not necessarily a person you already know. Many executives willingly share knowledge and contacts and are very co-operative if you make a well-reasoned request.

- The purpose of these conversations is not to get a job right away. It is to gain knowledge of the field and introduce yourself so they know who you are if a job opportunity were to open up later on. It is always helpful to be a familiar face.

- Ask for informational interviews with bosses to whom you look up. Occasionally you will be rejected, but so what? You have lost nothing. On the contrary, an informational interview is a way of expanding your network of contacts and maybe moving closer to your dream job.

- One fine day, you may be at the top of the ladder, and always remember then to give people who contact you a good reception.

EXERCISE:

1. *If you are job-hunting or considering a career change, imagine the dream scenario for your future work life.*

2. *What kind of business person would you like to speak to about gaining your dream job?*

3. *Arrange an informational interview with them to gain insight into the business and expand your network of contacts in the field.*

45. Coffee Meetings Are the New Black

- A coffee meeting is said to be a business date with the potential for a lot more: an informal way of meeting experts, listening to their insights and, within an hour, deciding if there is anything in it for you.

- This new trend is a great option if you run into someone at a meeting but are unable to assess whether or not this person could be a valuable contact. Or, if you have a contact to whom you would like to pay special attention or a relevant contact from whom you would like something.

- If the coffee meeting takes place at the other person's work place, you could bring some quality coffee, or you could invite him or her to a café. Find a place that suits your brand or the story you are going to tell about yourself and your business.

- There is an unwritten code of conduct for people who participate in coffee meetings. A very important rule is that it seldom takes more than an hour to "grab coffee". Another is that the whole set-up makes it a no-obligation meeting. It means that most business people find it easy to accept an invitation. A lunch or a dinner takes much longer and demands a higher level of commitment.

- How do you make the most of coffee meetings?
    - You are the one who invites and pays. Suggest a date, a time and a place.
    - Do your homework so you know about the person you are meeting and the key subjects you plan to bring up.
    - Create a positive atmosphere, show interest in the other person, and don't pitch or ask for a job at the first meeting.
    - Thank your guest for accepting your invitation.
    - Also thank him or her when you end the meeting (on time) no matter what came out of it. He or she may help you at a later time.

EXERCISE:

1. *Choose a contact who could be a part of your vision and invite him or her to a coffee meeting. Research how they could be helpful to you.*

2. *Do not ask for the impossible – be realistic in your requests expectations. Consider using the first meeting to generate rapport.*

3. *Work out how you could help and add value for your contact (see tip 21).*

46. SALON-STYLE NETWORKING

- A different way to use and gain value from your network is through networking salons.

- You invite 10-20 interesting professional people from different occupations and backgrounds. Four or five of these are asked to speak for a maximum of 10 minutes each. They are asked to talk on subjects about which they are passionate and can give inspiration to other participants. Sometimes the meetings are themed and the speakers are requested to address specific subjects.

- Salon-style meetings normally take two-to-three hours and may be organized as follows:
    - A short welcome and presentation of the guidelines of the meeting
    - The first speaker talks about one of his or her passions (10 min)
    - Questions and answers (10 min)
    - Second and third speakers on the same subject – same process
    - A 20-minute break during which people network. At this point,

the participants have a common platform and feel rather familiar with one another. This aids effective networking and promotes a positive atmosphere.

- After the break, the participants listen to the last few presentations

- At the end of the meeting the baton is passed on – who is going to host the next networking salon? The salons could, with some advantage, be continued with the same people, but it is critical to include new contacts so that the groups can grow and develop with different people and passions in the future networking salons.

EXERCISE:

1. *Establishing a networking salon is an effective way of revitalizing your network. Decide who are going to be participants, issue invitations, host the salon and be its chair. Run a session and participants will have a fantastic experience and build new relationships. You will be the overall winner.*

2. *It is critical that the speakers realize their talks should be written and performed so as to capture people's attention and interest. These talks are not about selling products and services. The speakers have a maximum of 10 minutes and are stopped if they exceed the time limit.*

3. *Hosting salon networking is, in itself, a rewarding networking exercise.*

47. VISIBILITY AND BUSINESS CARDS

- Have you tried to contact a person at a networking event and been fascinated by that person's competences and history? You exchange business cards and you are left with a small piece of paper printed at home. What are you thinking? Can you sustain your first impression of the person or is it falling apart?

- Cards, folders and websites are an extension of your personal brand. If they are not compatible with your business or you, contacts are going to question whether you are the person you say you are.

- Remember that the materials you hand out say a lot about you. Only give out materials of which you are proud when you meet important new contacts.

- Always bring along business cards containing relevant information:
  - The design and quality of the card should be first class as it communicates much about the quality of the company and you
  - A photo makes it easier to recall the person later
  - The back of the business card should be blank. Here the recipient can write notes and keywords

- Last but not least, a business card is a practical accessory that ensures the recipient receives all relevant contact information (name, job title, company name, phone number/s, email and website address). But if the cards are left in your pocket or in a holder, what is the use? Cards must be given out or they are of no value.

EXERCISE:

1. *Give your business cards and marketing materials a major overhaul. Are you happy with the way they represent you and your company? If not, this may be the right time for change.*

48. THE ELEVATOR PITCH

- In the world of business, it is very important to have a professional 'elevator pitch' prepared

- An elevator pitch, or story, is a very short speech lasting 30-90 seconds. The term 'elevator pitch' reflects the idea that in the short time it takes to ride an elevator, you should be able to give essential information about yourself:
  - Who are you?
  - What do you do for a living?
  - What are your plans?

- You always need to have an elevator pitch prepared when you take part in networking and business meetings. On these occasions, you are expected to introduce yourself and your qualifications, and people take turns, as it were, to deliver their pitches. The elevator pitch is also relevant in face-to-face interaction. It is important to adopt an informal conversation style so that the pitch does not seem to be an automated presentation.

- If your message is to be remembered, your elevator pitch should be simple (see tip 24). Concentrate on one message per pitch as the listener cannot relate to a wide range of information. Keep a number of elevator pitches in your portfolio – and give highest priority to the pitch that best suits your particular audience and situation.
    - Practise being authentic and passionate.
    - Use metaphors or stories that describe your passions or goals as these are what most people remember best.
    - Ensure your enthusiasm rubs off on your listeners so they want to hear more.
    - Practise at home so you feel comfortable with your pitch.
    - If possible, include an element of surprise. Most elevator pitches are formal and slightly boring, so this is where you could score "brownie points" with your conversation partners.

EXERCISE:

1. *Decide how many elevator pitches you need. One pitch – one message!*

2. *Make a note of keywords. Design your pitch.*

3. *Practise your delivery.*

4. *Include metaphors, stories and a surprise.*

5. *Hopefully, you are now looking forward to giving your elevator pitch.*

49. PREPARATIONS AND EXERCISES FOR NETWORKING

- Practise entering a gathering and decide how you want to be seen. Keep up with politics, the news, music and the latest styles in fashion. It boosts your self-confidence to be able to talk to anyone and everyone about a little bit of everything.

- Have three small talk questions prepared – and a good exit comment as well.

- Set goals for how many, and the kinds of, contacts you are going for.

- Remember to bring business cards and a pen and paper.

- Seek to make eye contact with other people, introduce yourself and ask wh-questions.

- Be an active listener and use follow-up questions. Try to identify common interests or passions.

- No guts, no glory! Take chances; do not wait for people to approach you.

- Do not forget to circulate.

- Be the best version of yourself.

- Always remember:
    - Find out what people want to achieve
    - Show them how they can do it
    - Everyone wants to feel appreciated
    - No one can resist enthusiasm and dedication
    - Praise works, flattery will take you nowhere
    - Say it as it is

EXERCISE:

After the meeting, evaluate your performance:

1. *Did you achieve your goals?*

2. *What would you do differently next time?*

3. *Praise yourself for what you achieved.*

50. SETTING PRIORITIES

- While reading this book, you have probably encountered tips that were more relevant to you than others – maybe for the simple reason that these tips identified your challenges.

- If you have a sincere wish to improve your networking competences and benefit fully from the discipline, it is not enough to read this book. The key to success is hands-on learning, or learning by doing. Set goals for how you implement the relevant tips.

- Make a list of the tips that seem most important for achieving your full potential.

EXERCISE:

1. Which tips are relevant to you?

_____

_____

_____

2. Which tips gave you a wider approach to networking? How can you use them in your everyday work and management?

_____

_____

_____

3. *Which tips inspired you to change routines? How are you going to implement the new routines?*

_____

_____

_____

4. *Which tips are you going to work on next week? Within the next month? How are you going to implement the tips and when? Make a detailed plan.*

_____

_____

_____

5. *What factors should be taken into consideration when you network in future?*

_____

_____

_____

LEARN TO NAVIGATE YOUR NETWORK CONSTRUCTIVELY

If you want to optimize your life – to exploit the full potential of your work life as well as your personal life – you need to connect with people.

If you do not have a good and relevant network, you will have to contact a lot of people and beg them to help you. This could be humiliating!

If you have an efficient network, a potential helper is already in your mind when you have a good idea or need assistance.

There is no one way to be the perfect networker. By discovering the authentic you combined with the helpful tips in this book you can create your personal unique way of networking.

ABOUT THE AUTHOR

SIMONE ANDERSEN is a journalist and has a Master's degree in media studies. She worked for many years at the Danish Broadcasting Corporation (DR) as an editor and talk show host. She is an expert in business networking and building relations. Simone has written several bestselling books and gives talks on these subjects.

CONTACT THE AUTHOR FOR ADVICE, TRAINING, OR SPEAKING OPPORTUNITIES:

sla@strategisk.dk - +45 26161818
www.thenetworkingcompany.com
www.strategisk.dk

ALSO BY THE AUTHOR:

- *Networking – Tør du lade være*/Publisher BoD (2014)
- *Networking – En professionel disciplin*/Publisher BoD (2011)
- *Få succes i netværk - via kropssprog, smalltalk og kultur*/Publisher BoD (2008)
- *Networking – a professional discipline*, 2nd edition:
  In English: http://bookboon.com/dk/networking-english-ebook
  In Swedish: http://bookboon.com/se/networking-svensk-ebook
  In Norwegian: http://bookboon.com/no/nettverking-ebook

years

building on our success

- 1993 Madrid
- 2007 Barcelona
- 2008 Mexico DF & Monterrey
- 2010 London
- 2011 New York & Buenos Aires
- 2012 Bogota
- 2014 Shanghai & San Francisco